Investigate

Life Cycles

Charlotte Guillain

Heinemann
LIBRARY

www.heinemann.co.uk/library

Visit our website to find out more information about Heinemann Library books.

To order:

☎ Phone 44 (0) 1865 888066

🖹 Send a fax to 44 (0) 1865 314091

💻 Visit the Heinemann Bookshop at www.heinemann.co.uk/library to browse our catalogue and order online.

Heinemann Library is an imprint of Pearson Education Limited, a company incorporated in England and Wales having its registered office at Edinburgh Gate, Harlow, Essex, CM20 2JE – Registered company number: 00872828

Edited by Sarah Shannon, Catherine Clarke, and Laura Knowles
Designed by Joanna Hinton-Malivoire, Victoria Bevan, and Hart McLeod
Picture research by Liz Alexander
Production by Duncan Gilbert
Originated by Chroma Graphics (Overseas) Pte. Ltd
Printed and bound in China by Leo Paper Group

ISBN 978 0 431932 71 2 (hardback)
12 11 10 09 08
10 9 8 7 6 5 4 3 2 1

ISBN 978 0 431932 90 3 (paperback)
13 12 11 10 09
10 9 8 7 6 5 4 3 2 1

British Library Cataloguing in Publication Data
Guillain, Charlotte
    Life cycles. - (Investigate)
    571.8
BA full catalogue record for this book is available from the British Library.

Acknowledgements
We would like to thank the following for permission to reproduce photographs: ©Corbis pp. **5**, **20** (Momatiuk–Eastcott), **7** (Frans Lanting), **18** (Andy Rouse), **29** (Richard Hamilton Smith); ©FLPA pp. **4** (Martin B Withers), **6** (Mitsuaki Iwago/Minden Pictures), **9** (Andrew Forsyth); ©Getty Images pp. **14** (Mike Parry), **15** (Bob Elsdale/The Image Bank), **21** (Eastcott Momatiuk/National Geographic), **23** (Louis Schwartzberg/Photographer's Choice), **24** (Greg Elms/StockFood Creative); ©istockphoto pp. **10** (Gertjan Hooijer), **11** (Sven Peter), **13** (Rob Sylvan), **26** (Alex Hinds); ©naturepl.com p. **17** (Anup Shah); ©NHPA p. **19** (Andy Rouse); ©Photolibrary pp. **8** (SUNSET PHOTO AGENCY), **12** (Francois Gilson/Photononstop), **16** (M HARVEY/ABPL), **22** (Oxford Scientific), **25** (Stephen Hamilton/Garden Picture Library), **27** (Juliette Wade /Garden Picture Library).

Cover photograph of Nile crocodile (Crocodylus niloticus) hatching from egg. Murchison Falls NP, Uganda, East Africa reproduced with permission of ©NaturePL (Bruce Davidson).

Every effort has been made to contact copyright holders of material reproduced in this book. Any omissions will be rectified in subsequent printings if notice is given to the publishers.

Contents

What is a life cycle?. 4

Ostriches 6

Frogs 10

Crocodiles. 14

Grizzly bears 18

Butterflies 22

Tomato plants 24

Comparing life cycles 28

Checklist 30

Glossary. 31

Index 32

Some words are shown in bold, **like this**. You can find out what they mean by looking in the glossary.

What is a life cycle?

A life cycle is the stages that an animal or plant goes through as it grows. Animal life cycles start with a tiny egg. The animal grows and changes until it is an **adult**.

Plant life cycles start with a **seed**. The plant grows from the seed. When the plant is fully grown it makes new seeds.

seeds

Ostriches

OSTRICH FACTS

➠ Ostriches are the largest birds in the world.

➠ Ostriches can run faster than any other bird.

➠ Ostriches cannot fly.

All birds **hatch** from eggs. The **female** birds lay eggs. Several female ostriches lay their eggs in one nest.

Q

Why do ostriches lay their eggs in nests?

? **CLUE**

• How does a nest keep the eggs safe?

A The eggs stay warm together in a nest. When the eggs are all together, the ostriches can take it in turns to watch them. They can stop other animals eating the eggs.

After about 40 days, the ostrich eggs **hatch** into chicks.

The ostrich chicks' parents look after them. The chicks eat leaves, **roots**, flowers, and **seeds** to grow. When the chicks are three or four years old, they have grown into **adult** ostriches. The female adults can make their own eggs.

Frogs

Amphibians live partly in water and partly on land. Frogs, toads, and newts are amphibians. **Female** frogs lay their eggs in water in the spring.

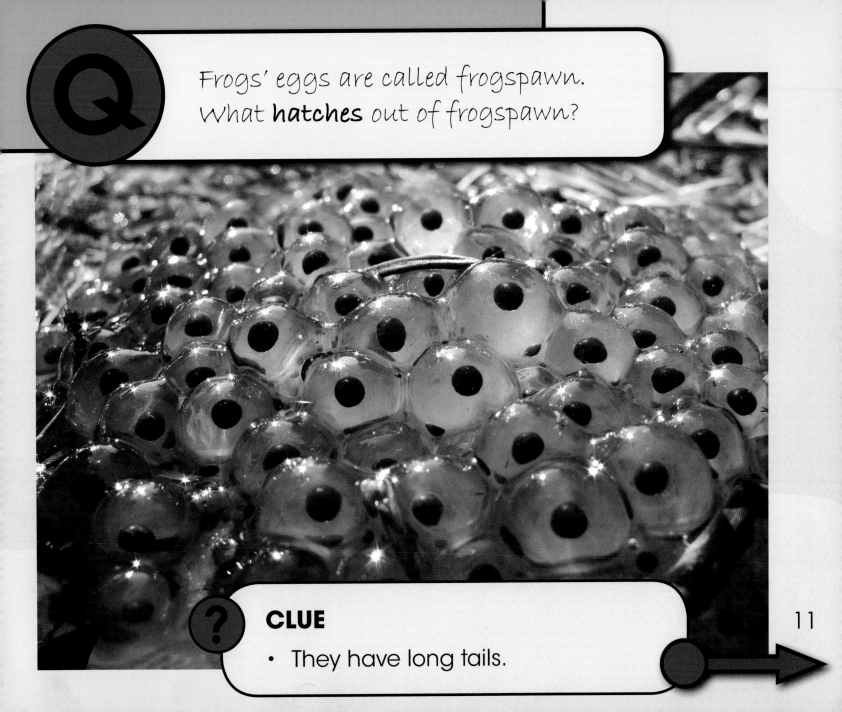

Q Frogs' eggs are called frogspawn. What **hatches** out of frogspawn?

? **CLUE**
• They have long tails.

A The frogspawn hatches into tadpoles.

Tadpoles live in water and use their tails to swim. They eat plants to grow bigger and grow legs.

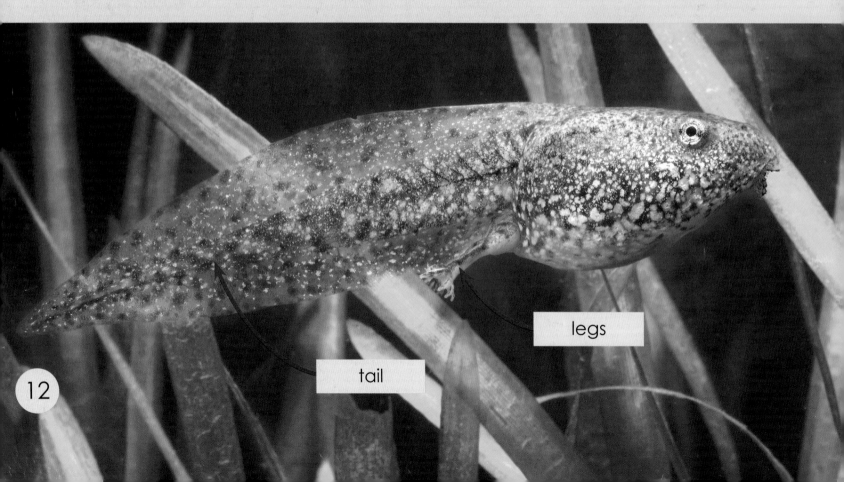

legs

tail

12

The tadpole changes into a froglet. It grows four legs. Its tail is much smaller. The froglet can live on water and land, and starts to eat **insects**. When a **female** has grown into an **adult** frog, it can make its own eggs.

Crocodiles

Reptiles have **scales**, and most lay eggs. Crocodiles are reptiles. They live in water and on land. They can stay under water for up to fifteen minutes.

The saltwater crocodile is the largest reptile in the world.

Female crocodiles lay their eggs on land.

Q

How do baby crocodiles get out of the eggs?

? **CLUE**
• They use part of their body.

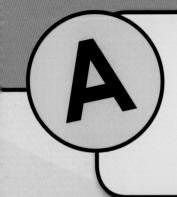

A The baby crocodiles have an egg tooth on their nose to chip their way out of the egg. They make a grunting noise so their mother knows they are **hatching**.

egg tooth

The mother crocodile looks after the baby crocodiles. Sometimes she will carry them to the water in her mouth. Baby crocodiles eat **insects** and fish to grow. After about ten years they have grown into **adults**. The female adults can make their own eggs.

Grizzly bears

Mammals are animals that have warm blood, hair on their bodies, give birth to live young, and feed their babies with milk. Bears, elephants, kangaroos, dolphins, mice, and even humans are all mammals.

An egg grows inside a **female** bear. When this happens the mother bear is **pregnant**. She can be pregnant for 3 to 8 months.

Q Do bears lay eggs?

CLUES

- Bears are mammals.
- Do other mammals, such as humans, lay eggs?

A Bears do not lay eggs. The mother gives birth to a baby bear. A baby bear is called a cub. It stays close to its mother and drinks her milk.

← Female bears normally have two cubs at a time.

The cubs stay with their mother for two or three years. They eat berries, plants, fish, **insects**, and other small animals to grow. After about five years they have grown into an **adult**. They can then make their own babies.

Butterflies

Butterflies are **insects**. Butterflies lay their eggs on plants. A caterpillar **hatches** out of each egg. The caterpillar eats plants and grows.

A female adult butterfly can lay its own eggs.

When it is fully grown, the caterpillar hangs upside down and its skin comes off. Under the caterpillar's skin is the **chrysalis**. This is a hard case that keeps the caterpillar safe. The caterpillar changes into a butterfly inside the chrysalis. Then the butterfly comes out of the chrysalis.

23

Tomato plants

The tomatoes we eat grow on a plant. You can see the **seeds** inside a tomato. Tomato plants grow from these seeds.

Seeds start to grow in spring. They need water and sunlight to grow.

Q What happens to a seed when it is planted?

CLUE
- What grows out of the seed?

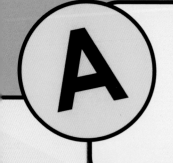

First a **root** grows out of the seed. It pushes down into the ground. After one or two weeks a shoot grows up from the seed. The shoot pushes up through the soil into the sunlight.

shoot

roots

 The roots hold the plant in the soil and suck up water from the soil.

The plant gets bigger and grows leaves. When the plant is tall enough it grows flowers. Then tomatoes grow. At first the tomatoes are green but they slowly turn red. Inside the tomatoes there are seeds to grow more plants.

TOMATO FACT

➠ Tomatoes are fruits, not vegetables.

Comparing life cycles

Living thing	What is it?	How does the life cycle start?	What does it need to grow?
ostrich	bird	Male and **female** mate. Female lays eggs.	Parents look after the chicks. They eat leaves, **roots**, flowers, and **seeds**.
frog	**amphibian**	Male and female mate. Female lays eggs.	Tadpoles eat plants. Froglets eat **insects**.
crocodile	**reptile**	Male and female mate. Female lays eggs.	Baby crocodiles need their mother to look after them. They eat insects and shellfish.
grizzly bear	**mammal**	Male and female mate. Female becomes **pregnant** and gives birth to baby or babies.	Cubs need their mother to look after them and feed them milk.
butterfly	insect	Male and female mate. Female lays eggs.	Caterpillars eat plants.
tomato plant	plant	A seed is planted in the soil.	Water and sunlight.

All mammals need their mothers to look after them because their mother provides their food when they are babies.

All living things have different life cycles. They all grow and change in different ways. They can all make new animals or plants.

Checklist

A life cycle is the stages an animal or a plant goes through as it grows.

Animal life cycles start with an egg.

Plant life cycles start with a **seed**.

Some animals lay eggs. Some animals give birth to babies.

Some animals need their parents when they are young. Some animals do not need their parents.

All animals need food to grow and change into **adults**.

Glossary

adult fully grown, or grown-up

amphibian animal that can live in water and on land

chrysalis hard case in which a caterpillar changes into a butterfly

female animal that can have babies or lay eggs

hatch come out of an egg

insect tiny animal that has six legs and usually two pairs of wings

mammal animal that feeds its babies on milk

pregnant when a female animal is carrying a growing baby inside her

reptile animals that have scales

root part of a plant that grows under the ground

scales small plate on an animal's body. Animals with scales have them all over their body instead of skin or fur.

seed new plants grow from seeds

Index

amphibians 10, 28

birds 6–9, 28

chrysalis 23

egg tooth 16
eggs 4, 7–10, 14–16,
    19–20, 22

frogspawn 11

insects 13, 17, 22, 28

mammals 18–19, 28–29

nests 7–8

plants 5, 12, 21–22, 24,
    28

reptiles 14, 28

seeds 5, 24-27

tadpoles 12–13